Dead Man's Quintet

Poems

Thomas Zimmerman

ISBN: 978-81-19228-89-8

First Edition: 2023
Rs. 200/-

Cyberwit.net
HIG 45 Kaushambi Kunj, Kalindipuram
Allahabad - 211011 (U.P.) India
http://www.cyberwit.net
Tel: +(91) 9415091004
E-mail: info@cyberwit.net

Printed at Vcore.

Acknowledgments

The author thanks the editors of the following publications, where these poems first appeared, sometimes in earlier versions:

Adaptations, *The Beautiful Space*, *Breathe Bold*, *Crossing Borders*, *Ephemeral Elegies*, *Fahmidan Journal*, *Goat's Milk Magazine*, *Going Viral*, *Grand Little Things*, *Green Ink Poetry*, *The Green Silk Journal*, *hand picked poetry*, *Haven Speculative*, *HerStory*, *Interstellar Literary Review*, *Jasper's Folly Poetry Journal*, *Live Nude Poems*, *Making Herstory*, *Many Nice Donkeys*, *The Minison Project: Sonnet Collection Series* (Vol. 3, 4, and 5), *Moonchild Magazine*, *Origins*, *Pages Literary Journal*, *The Paper Crow*, *Peace and War*, *Pink Plastic House*, *Pulsebeat Poetry Journal*, *The Rail*, *Revolver*, *Roi Fainéant Press*, *Rough Diamond Poetry Journal*, *Sage Cigarettes*, *Shadow*, *Sixpence Society*, *Sledgehammer*, *Spellbinder*, *Summer Reading*, *Superfroot*, *These Lines*, *Tistelblomma*, *TMP Magazine*, *Trestle Ties*, *Trigger Warning*, *The Unconventional Courier*, *Yellow Mama*, *Zero Readers*.

Cover image and author photograph by the author.

Contents

I.

Atlas

We've fed the dog and spread the final bags
of mulch out back. I've cracked a beer, of course.
Now Thumper, Dad's old pasta pot, is rocking
on the stovetop. He's been dead . . . how long?
Mom, also gone, collapses time: "I push
you out. And now . . . around. Suck in your gut."
I see our neon lights for Halloween—
a purple skull, an arch-backed cauldron cat—
lie deadly on the kitchen table. Your
HGTV fixation holds. An Atlas
of my own imagination, I
am ruptured holding up my world. Inside
or out, fair weather darkens with my fate.
Am I the same young self that ate my shadow?
Pop psychology. God's love is crushing
me. Dark angel smiles: "Survive this. Try."

Bach's First Cello Suite

We'll wake tomorrow altered, recombined
with glues and acids of our dreams, the same
old carcasses, just older, hours closer
to a death. Not ours. The we that's us
will fly or fall or whirl somewhere, some rare
dimension, deep within or far beyond
this space. It's why we strive. Our deeds, they're bound
within this page or screen, but ripple out
for anyone who sees them with attention
and compassion. Bach is on the playlist now:
first cello suite, the tones a human voice
that reaches us three centuries away,
and glowing sunset lights our shaggy backyard
spruces, candles burning green and growing.

Blowing Smoke

When I play my dad's old record albums—
Waylon Jennings, Willie Nelson—
I smell his cigarette smoke in the sleeves.
I smell it too in his leather bomber jacket
I've worn for 15 years. A little long for me:
he stood 6'1"; I got my mother's height.
Smoke killed her: emphysema
after five decades of two packs a day.
They had her on oxygen near the end.
On the rest-home patio,
my sister and I would yank the tubes,
light one up (the nurses knew she kept a stash),
and let her puff till her lips turned blue.

I was stoned to the point of vertigo
the night I met the woman who would be my wife.
I saw it only darkly.
When we lived in North Dakota,
I swear I swallowed smoke one time:
squatting over the portable grill,
bratwursts sizzling, skin cracking,
wind 30 miles an hour, bellyache just short of puking.
I remember a crop duster coming in,
horizon line miles away.
Topsoil from the sugar-beet fields
like brown smoke suspended in air,
tractors tearing the veil from Earth.

Box of Thoughts

The beer I drink is bitter but without
much character: like friends we've had and lost
or dropped. My wife's on Zoom, the dog's asleep,
and I am stranded with my thoughts: a monkey mind
that swings from tree to tree, then beats its chest
or scratches its bare ass. Thank goodness for
the music: Shostakovich, tragic with
some jokes thrown in. Great art beats death, and life.
The sky is darkening, it looks like rain.
The backyard spruces rage like shaggy mammoths
in the wind. Just thought I saw my double,
long-haired, clawed, and hunkered on all fours.
Raccoon, I realize now. It's shredding something.
Book I left outside. My poems, of course.

Casarecce

Eleven minutes till al dente, so
the package says. And Thumper, Dad's old pasta
pot, has been hot only two. There's time
to crack a second beer, and get a little
meta: homemade poems make me feel
alive. I try to do my best right now,
not worry over what will happen after
death. It's Pink Floyd on the playlist: spacy
terror, softcore emotion, retro fun.
Telling heaven from hell? Unimportant
now. But later? Strange how music, movies,
verse can bring that throat lump, open what
we think is closed. Like found notes for a memoir
still unfinished. Rain prayed for all day.

Confluence

A pint of stout in front of me and Bruckner
in my ear. Today the sunshine broke
a string of seven days of ashen clouds.

Imagine inspiration, sense its old
confluence: energy, materials,
and time. Sublime symphonic slabs of sound.

And it's a crossroads too: the witch
in me that dallies there casts shadow—
but the spells will come. And in my mind's eye,

Trey and I—black dog, white man—are toiling
up a path that forks, a gleaming sunbeam
—no, a bolt of lightning—overhead.

Driving Home

A Coltrane solo's
loping from
the stereo.

The GPS
keeps chiding, "Route
recalculating."

The music fills
my head and chest.

I feel the sky
is opening.

Wrong turns are now
my specialty.

Essay on Frameworks

I love a frame: it measures and contains.
I also like a gap in it: a cell door,
exit (entrance) for the maze. I feel
this way with people too: give everyone
a safety net, an easy out. A framework
lets us dream of order we can know.
But there's a larger, subtler order we
can't see beyond the frame: imagined chaos.
Entropy: things fall apart. The putting-
back-together: that's our pleasure and
salvation. These new frames can tell us where
to stop but also to go back, to add
the necessary brushstrokes, stoke the inner
light, to make the framework not a prison
but a portal searchers walk through freely:
and, if not reborn, at least refreshed.

Everblue

It's here, my yearly birthday bleed. The everblue
mood descends upon me—or ascends,
from depths of riches I don't understand.
A darting shark among a shoal, my focus
shifts, to drinks outside last night with friends:
for Sandy, Fran, and Ann, champagne; and beer
for Gary and me. Cool eastern breeze that bore
our laughter, hell, as far as Iowa.
Epiphanies? Yes. Other people give
life meaning. Treat myself as friend (and realize
why I keep on typing *fiend*). Blue eyes
I got from Mom (from Dad, the gold explosions
near the pupils). Wish my darker sister
happy Mother's Day, belatedly.

Family Matters

Trauma, drama, dream. These family matters
more familiar to me from movies or
TV. What did I miss? A plane flying over

the Mediterranean, the cabin losing
pressure, the paper cup covering my nose
and mouth, funneling oxygen. The airport

in Athens, Mom buying me a keychain with
a miniature harmonica attached.
Earlier, in Frankfurt, Jean-Marie

and I running the bases, round and round,
at Dad's army-post softball field, she
afraid a plane would land on her head. Later,

Ankara, me entering the house of Turkish
friends, rose water sprinkled on me gets
in my eyes, I cry. And later still, it's Christine

in an oxygen tent, her baby teeth
bared, rotten brown from all the medicines.
Why does my mind leap, hurt animal?

Last night I dreamed I met a coyote in
the woods, I thought it would fear me, run away,
but no, it came on, bristling, grimacing,
fanged, and fierce. My waking saved my life.

Flock

The drink might kill me: I don't care.
I type a word, I tilt my tone of voice
to reach someone I think will need it.

There's so little concrete here:
a black keyboard, my stubbled jowls,
dishwasher churning tides inside itself.

"Be the river and the boulder
in the river." Stole it from a friend.
He wants to know what happens after death.
Which means he's wondering how to live.

Last night, three couples on the deck:
strong beers, champagne, and birthday cake:
we're in our 60s, so we think we know
a portion of the world
(and some of us think bigger).

Money makes a difference,
but that warm space between the ears,
where love or winged compassion shelters,
it's a universe, and we flock there.

Forecast

Long misty day ahead. New age-spots on
my veiny hand-backs. Baggy eyes. The smile
lines, harbingers of jowls. Just maybe, when
the storm kicks up, I'll do my Lear, get naked,
howl along. A bare forked animal,
in need. But now, I hear a plate clank in
the kitchen, scrape of knife on toast. Downstairs,
my wife flips through a catalog: my mind's
eye sees her lick her middle finger. A friar,
local news this morning says, will be
beatified today. A plane, or thunder,
rumbles overhead. The backyard spruce
trees sway, so dark, so deep: the way they keep
their green a minor miracle. Small beads
of rain now tremble all along the eaves.

Heavy

It's all these years piled heavily: a stacked
deck shuffled, dealt: a fate. No wonder that
my shoulders slope, my middle's spread. I build
a house of cards: the woman that I think
I want. I tower all my quarters: manhood
I've been fed. Yes, I could take it to
the river, old-time song and faith. A bluesman's
there, waist-deep in water, fingerpicking
a guitar, his cab parked back behind
the buckthorn-strangled scrub, his singing achy-
sweet, his neck: taut cords and well-worn leather.
"Be like him," I tell myself, but we
must meet to share our stories. Wide and deep,
the water. Heavy with the years, my legs.

The Last Word

The turkey bolognese is cooked, just needs
reheating: much like me. I've cut my world
to bite-sized chunks and hashed the other parts
so smooth that I can try them with a spoon.
Beethoven's Third, with Otto Klemperer,
my favorite, conducting, blares bright from
the speaker, grabs my spirit by its frayed
lapels, and shakes the bullshit out. Almost.
There's often just a little despot left,
Napoleon on Elba. Teacher, poet,
brother, husband: fetishes I relish,
though I sometimes lack my mother's cast-iron
stomach for. I'm sixty-one: prime number,
hardly prime of life. Oh, Tom. Relax.

Late Afternoon in Early Spring

Sun's finally out,
like God, or someone,
took the lid off the pot
we've been steeping in.
We can breathe.
Finish your tea,
we'll walk the dog
and let our looser
molecules drift into
the trees and clouds
and not-so-distant river:
our re-entry
into the swirling
elemental world.

Listening to Bach's Violin

Sonata No. 2,
the music's sinews stretch
my mind to open up
a space for grace and calm
acceptance. This is nothing

new in theory, but
each time it happens is
a revelation. Trees
outside my office window,
filtered sunlight, breath

inside my head, sweet
candle smell, my wife's
key-clatter: data of
the moment noted, swirling
in the psyche, lived.

Making Tacos

July, just dusk, and muggy as hell. Thank God
the central air still works. I've shredded chicken,
mixed in black beans, onions, peppers, cumin.
Heating it to meld the flavors. Ann's
upstairs on Zoom, and Trey's zonked in the living
room. The warm dishwasher's gurgle swirls
below my Coltrane playlist. Did I mention
that I'm drinking beer? You know: it helps.
I wish for little more than what I have.
Desire is the root of all our suffering,
right? We try to simplify ourselves
to nothing. Fine. But it's impossible.
If we're alive, there's human residue:
A smooth then screechy streaming saxophone.
Aroma from the frying pan. This poem.

Nineteen Lines on Ancestry

My youngest sister's into ancestry:
we're German, Irish, Danish, mostly. Dad
and Mom had told us that. The geek in me,
now three beers in, is paddling back to Hamlet,
barking mad in Denmark's rot. Love glows
so wanly from his words. The Ghost, his father,
goads him (Why do I keep typing "gods him"?).
Now Olivier's popped up, bleach-blond,
theatrical: our funhouse-mirrored GIFs
disintegrate and shift. The silver screen?
Urn ash. So exeunt to '66,
with Dad in Vietnam, and Mom and I,
up watching TV late: it's *Waiting for
Godot*, Mostel and Meredith a blur,
my sisters long asleep. Ah, violins!
A playlist Haydn string quartet has slipped
me back to me: I'm sixty, time-warped, tipsy,
smiling at the nighttime window's rain-streaked
face I try to take a selfie of.

Nocturne (III)

Hard rain this afternoon with drops so big
they came down white. Just sprinkling now: I see
the dimpling puddles on the deck. It's reruns
of *The Office* on TV, and Creed's
just cracked a joke about some sprouts he's grown:
"nutritious, but they smell like death." Like all
that's wet outside: the blood-brown mulch, the spruces
shaggy as the mastodons that went
extinct 12,000 years ago. The brain-haze
from this beer, my third, has blurred the data,
darkened passing time. A retro vibe
tonight, for sure, with Pink Floyd in one ear,
and Thumper, Dad's old pasta pot, now rocking
on the stovetop. Bubbles rising, just
to die. The same old fears. Wish you were here.

Nondominant Hand: A Fragment

My dad went ambidextrous after Vietnam:
a mortar shell hit near his jeep and broke
his shoulder. Mom drew pigs and dogs (but never
horses) with her left, a cigarette
pinched in her right. My sisters, lefties both.
And I've slugged with my right hand all my life:
my left is bigger though. I see Mom's soft
hands now: her long white fingers stained old gold
with nicotine. She never got to San
Francisco. I've gone for her, worked it out
in half-assed poems. "Never wanted kids,"
she used to say, smoke jetting from the corner
of her mouth. "A free spirit's what I should
have been." My dad lived milder, rubbing lotion
in his hands at night: the letters he
delivered daily sucked the oil out.
And two beers in, he'd joke and wave those hands
like great beige birds. No, don't say mourning doves.

A Piece Retrievable

Election Night 2020

I've used these thousand poems as a record:
not the whole of any life, yet each
a piece retrievable, a broken funhouse
mirror shard that cuts unless it's fingered

gently. Chicken flautas in the oven,
lettuce crisping in the fridge. A fifth
of whiskey on the counter, shadow long
as any bishop's on a chessboard. "Check

for brownness," reads a frozen-pizza box
in the recycling bin. My wife has gone
to bed, swing states a lullaby, a hammock

on a restive night. Outside the sliding
door, an ocean's swallowed all the world:
the kitchen hardwood sways beneath my feet.

William Blake and the Ephemeral

Strains in any marriage.
Even that of Heaven and Hell.
Ask Blake. His wife once said,
"I have very little

of Mr. Blake's company;
he is always in Paradise."
A framed Blake print,
The Great Red Dragon and

the Woman Clothed with Sun,
is hanging in our powder room.
We're hanging on.
I've told myself for years

to be in love with love.
And Blake might help:
"I do not consider either
the just, or the wicked,

to be in a supreme state,
but to be, every one of them,
states of the sleep
which the soul may fall into."

Sweet dreams. Be patient, kind,
and soon we'll wake.

Window on War

My father fought in Vietnam; Korea
too, where Uncle Dave got killed.
                                        I couldn't
pass the eye exam to get me to
West Point.
            My bedside book's Euripides:
the Trojan War the backdrop of so many
Attic tragedies.
                These thoughts explode
then dissipate like smoke: my podcast Buddhist
tells me they're not real.
                              But Putin's army's
real for people in Ukraine. There's war
in Ethiopia, Myanmar, Syria,
and COVID's wounded everyone.

Aboard a train one time, a colleague
told me war's a natural phenomenon:
like weather, there's no stopping it.
                                        Right now,
my office window shows me sunny breeze
and trees in bloom. How long before a storm?

II.

Business

Fine mist, as if a cloud were sitting on
the ground. Leaves, twigs, and branches underfoot.
Trey straining at the leash, a universe
of scents beyond his earthbound snout. A trail
can be a trial: I dodge a jutting root,
a branch knocks off my cap. It could be worse:
that time a skunk sprayed Scarlet; Percy gone
on strike in summer heat, his pace a snail's.
Those two long dead, their ashes still at home.
We need to scatter some in places that
they loved: the woods, a favorite evergreen.
My business is the living. What I mean
is movement, flux. Now Trey's just seen a cat—
a flash—it's disappeared. And so's this poem.

Canyon Echoes

Tonight, I duel life—to prove my love
for it. The sonnet is my sword of choice.
Meal cooked, a second beer in front of me,
my wife upstairs on Zoom. Beethoven on
the playlist: middle string quartets. Above
those violins, viola, cello—voice
of gods, or human striving. Form can free
our arts and deeds from quick extinction. Dawn
breaks anytime. The light shines brighter in
this dark deluxe sublet called middle age.
No kids, no heirs. But thinning hair. Begin
and end in gratitude, today's blond sage
might offer. Canyon echoes, the belief
that feelings matter. Love's full price is grief.

Cartography

These hands that span the pastel lands of maps:
they're veined with rivers, blue and red, and each
is christened *Thomas*, flow of doubt that laps
the shores of stolid fact, that grinds the beach,
that carves the mountain pass, that scoops and scours
the bays and lakes. It's ambiguity
of which I speak, I think: the gods' and ours,
complexity that shears fatuity.

We try to plot the known and unknown shapes
that crowd our dreams, our waking, racing minds,
our womb-time and the soundtrack trauma tapes
replaying while we measure, draw the blinds,
project our need and want, a craft and art
that tells a human story, cleaves the heart.

Chamber Music

And through my earbuds now, a string quartet:
King Lear, by Philip Glass. A tragic play
translated to the moans the bows beget
upon the strings: a humming midwife, say;
a groaning mom-to-be; or workmen's saws
at fragrant pine-planks for a coffin. Odd
these ecstasies of thought, these ravens' caws
that slice the mind's dark woods, with nightfall clawed
by stars like fiery demons straining to
break through. Our suffering's immense as space,
as planets dying in the blood. Our true
catharsis, birthed from tragedy: to face
the aged raving king, the children cruel,
the hero traumatized, reduced to fool.

Dreaming Phoenix

Gilt-edged horizon, dimming western sky.
My mind spins east with Earth. Rebirth. Red dawn
among the Mongols. Pharaohs rise and set
to stretch their wingspans over history.
The Ottomans and czars glow gold as rye.
The shoguns and the Trojan kings ride, drawn
by stallions bright as embers. Minaret,
pagoda, pyramid: their mystery
breathes out patchouli, lavender, and musk.
Computer snore and cellphone wheeze can't mar
my reverie. I've come unstuck in time.
My psyche's stoked and lit, my body's husk
sleeps, wrapped in tissue made for flight. Bright star
and moon alike rain light as old as rhyme.

First Coffee Break

The lo-fi groove of air conditioning
cocoons me in this dream of work. The floor-
to-ceiling windows are partitioning
a forest full of pines and spruces—more,
almost, than eyes can take, but green's a balm
mysterious and wild. My mind takes flight,
above the trees, in summer haze, breeze calm
as Buddhist emptiness, a second sight
that blinds me to illusion if I still
my monkey mind to clear pure space between
my thoughts and feelings, brute-force act of will
that scatters spirit-haunters, gulls that keen
insanity of anger, fear, desire,
inversion of the sun's life-giving fire.

From Memory

for MJZ (1939-2009)

Dad wouldn't let her work outside the home.
She taught me how to cook, arrange food on
a plate, enunciate, say "Thank you," comb
my hair. An Elvis fan, she'd dance till dawn,
but only if she thought it proper. Smoked
two packs a day but didn't drink until
her forties. Spent her last years vodka-soaked.
MS deep-fried her mind but not her will.
A Charlestown kid, she hated the Midwest
and kept her accent pure. She drew. She joked
Dad liked her best in red. But she preferred
light blue. These details of her life I wrest
from memory: a story blurred, and yoked
to guilt. But also love. Yes, that's the word.

Garden Muse

This morning, our designer brought us pied
red garden flowers that she said she'd trimmed.
We broke a wineglass Friday night, and sighed,
"Oh well, we're down to two." My mind, salt-rimmed
with pixelated daydreams I suppress,
is swizzling two parts Us and one part Grand
Design to make the cocktail: Eden. "Dress
it with a cherry," sings my Muse. "Then hand
the laptop over." Under laden trees,
we're all abuzz with spirits, knowledge next,
and then our nakedness. We're on our knees. . . .
My Muse clicks *God*, then *sex*, in hypertext—
Our paradise goes Poof! Alone, I'm left
with one line more. And now a word: *Bereft*.

Horses in the Dark

The water rushing in, a tide, a flood—
unconscious mind. I dive, dream-lathered now,
my conscience sparking blue despite the blood
that flushes me, the wet that weeps, and—wow!—
I've been asleep so many years. I lean
against the darkness, let it straddle me
to spur, to gouge—my ass, my back, my spleen.
Like being broken in the dark. The sea-
tossed spume on moon-stung sand's a bright white mane.
The hoof-kick's quick and dashes out the brain—
We prance in rain that sluices all the shit-
clogged gutters clean. Parisians ride gas-lit
above the catacombs. We hail Baudelaire,
who promises he'll take us anywhere.

Let's Call It

The last day of the world, a time to count
mixed blessings. Guilt and resolutions mount.

A lone voice in an empty room. Most thought
is this. God, too, the way the elders taught.

No, wait. The room is not so empty: there,
in shadow, bare as doubt, a wooden chair.

The floor's scrubbed clean, the window has no shade.
The muse is worried: "Where's the mess you made?"

Raindrops meander down the pane, like streams
that feed the rivers, and the tears, of dreams.

Let's call it "World's-End Sonnet No. 1":
the breeze has calmed, the rain is almost done.

Things pass . . . into the past . . . to disappear.
Memory reconstructs them, drags them here.

Midlife (VI)

A beer in front of me, wife blogging; dog
whines, shakes himself: all's well so far this year.
Rereading '60s poets: verses log
in code the months, days, hours, and minutes dear
to consciousness. Creation is the act
surpassing all, and if the poem's not
so good, just write another. Mind's intact
for now: I leave my record, Rorschach blot
a reader might interpret freely. When
it's published, it's no longer mine: just ink
or pixel, drowning silence, crowding space,
awaiting entropy's too-warm embrace.
Buck up, I tell myself. Still time to think
and feel before rebirth comes round again.

The Only Failure

The wind-tossed spruces: shaggy mastodons
still grazing. Raising ageless heads, they gaze
at me, zoo specimen, a poet. Days
and years drift by my office window, lawn's
choked out by ivy, clouds drag ragged hands
across the forehead of the daytime moon.
I'll cover all the bathroom mirrors soon:
the torso's hourglass, muscles' shifting sands.

Been passively resisting wisdom all my life,
though poems show the only failure is
the failure of imagination. Quiz
me in my guise as sage, or ask my wife:
no answers, only propositions; sketch
instead of portrait; thoughts just playing fetch.

Richard's Bones

Bones Under Parking Lot Belonged to Richard III
The New York Times, *February 4, 2013*

Discovery of Richard's bones below
that Leicester parking lot has made me think
about my own: A tuneless violin
within a battered case? A stand of pines
on fire in Wyoming? Scabs of snow
along I-94 as night turns pink?
To kill a king as sacrificial sin—
to plump the ears of wheat, to feed the vines,
to purge the plague—necessitates a myth
that comforts us, that renders Bosworth Field
Elysian: we must rise from death. And with
these thoughts I read myself to dreams each night:
sleep's darker sister might arrive, a slight
sting in her kiss, then all my ills die, healed.

So Tonight

you're telling me we live too safe. I flip
the atlas pages. Kiss? You smile, backstabs
and paper cuts are smiling back. Our code
post-post-ironic, half-forgotten songs.
Remember that we're blurry, visions slip
along our shimmer. Hisses, dots, and dabs
we cannot sense are painting us. This road
that's paved with useless dollars, dreamt-up wrongs?
I'll take the wheel, it's better in the ditch.
Here's what we'll do: decide what we're about,
relate these findings to a larger world,
and fashion them to last. We'll have to hitch
our pants up, chill beneath our shadowed doubt,
unpack our dreams: there, reborn We lies curled.

Stay Weird

A string quartet is humming through my ear-
buds: Glass's #4. I've played the 1,
the 2, the 3, their beauty tinged with fear,
sublime sound-mountains that can touch the sun,
reminding me that human striving staves
off entropy. Stay weird, we tell ourselves:
embrace but bend our cage. When Dylan raves
against the gentle and the light, twin elves
that cleave my mind reveal that I've misquoted
him. This morning in the woods, a fox
stopped in my path, between the roots and rocks:
I swear it read my darkness. "Dully noted,"
cawed a crow perched high above us. Wing-
thuds. Then a finch, unseen, began to sing.

Vacation

So, it's lasagna and *King Lear* tonight,
my wife retiring early with a book
on positive psychology, the light
of reason and right attitude the hook
lodged in her jaw. My metaphor yields death
and life, extinction and prosperity,
with fish and water—symbols—giving breath,
I think, to richer thoughts. Austerity
abides. To hell with it for now! I'm on
vacation. No more essays left to grade,
I nudge my mind to deeply dive, to spawn
in darkest depths, to breach with gifts inlaid
with opulence that sparkles under sun
and stars, that glitters as the currents run.

III.

Bleeding Bite-Sized Pieces

You've cracked a beer, thank God: it's Arrogant
Bastard, a favorite. Your wife's asleep,
TV's on mute. Poetic moment? So
you hope. You've worked all day at paycheck work.
And now, your heart's-blood work, your need to leave
a record. Music streaming from your playlist:
Shostakovich string quartet. The sonnet
and the blackout poem: twin crutches you've
been gimping on. You squirm, the thought-worm bores.
Right: lying fallow is a lie. The dog's
awake and biting on a squeaky toy. Sounds so
much like your verse. You dice a ripe tomato,
world that lies in bleeding bite-sized pieces.
Oh, what title ever captures this?

Fighting Off the Wise

Since life's at last smoothed out for him, he thinks
his sullen art should have more bite. And damned
Chopin is on the stereo again.
The major keys can make a person feel
a fresh world's breeze and birdsong, pulse and breath.
The minor, though, they shade the shadow, dim
the dark. He finds this richer, deeper, strange,
a mate for his persona, fighting off
the wise. He contemplates his latest sketch:
a long-necked woman, dark hair parted down
the middle, forehead creased and eyebrows thick.
Eyes close-set, large, and ringed by . . . grief? ennui?
fatigue? The mouth, however, full-lipped, smiling.
Oh to tear the page to shreds. He can't.

Glance

It's like a book, a piece of music: glance
from someone you believe is beautiful.
In fifty-mile-per-hour wind, or under
skies as white as Grandpa's thighs, the fire-core
of this vision burns. A Beethoven late
quartet, those fine brown eyes: the soul expands
as if put on a ventilator. Even
if you're diving into darkness (luxury
it is compared to falling), reading Lowell
or Plath, let's say, the alchemy of pure
delight transmutes the words and rhythms into
his or her or their remembered face,
now lovelier, of course, full moon seen underwater
as you're rising breathless from the depths.

Instead of Bad News

She pours some coffee, pets the dog,
and holds him off with snacks until
her second cup. The headlines crawl
across the bottom of the TV
screen: it's murder, scandal, mostly
cloudy, and Dow Jones. "I will
not waste my life," she tells herself.
"I'm finding meaning; giving and
receiving love." Her irony
ambiguous as Lilith myths.
The coffee's gone, it's still damn cold
outside: 16 degrees. She clicks
the dog leash, zips up tight: full armor
for a skirmish with the world.

Island Saga

1

What's happened on the island of your heart?
The queen has hanged herself?
The king's torn out his eyes?
Your children scatter,
exiles smart enough to sense
a fate accursed,
the rout of free will,
frail spine snapped against a
grim alignment of the stars.
And yet they act.
They suffer, learn, and now return,
like slim shoots in the fields,
like truth that outlasts fact.

2

She drinks strong wine,
and rhythmic words she needs
transform her.
Sea and sky,
and she a maid escaped,
a smoking fortress leagues behind her,
sharks below.
She plies the rudder,
freed to drown,
not contemplating death,
not brave,
just spying land,
soul bared to what she'll find.

Labyrinth

She puts a record on, a scratchy thing,
some Haydn string quartets, a thrift-shop steal,
a Mahler and a Beethoven among
the haul. More clutter for the house, but comfort
for the mind. Or the emotions. Oh,
OK: the soul. But why is it so hard
for her to say such things? Yes, irony
can ring as false as earnestness. There's nothing
false about the music. Lighter than
she'd like, but she could use some sun. Root-pale
and growing gnarlier, she twists infinity
into a peanut shell. Dark matter,
this. The needle's found its way to freedom.
Now the labyrinth spins silently.

Lonesome Road

The Zoom-screen mirror: sick of it. You've popped
a cork, the water's on the boil. Ricotta,

peas, prosciutto: check. The parsley ready
to be chopped, the pappardelle raw

and waiting: like a wedding night. Your '90s
indie playlist: fine, you've mixed in Joni,

Billie, Ella. Nights like this, the shaped
quotidian might morph its cells, its selves,

and recombine to terrify. Relax,
you tell yourself. We dream departures and

arrivals: flame-wheels burning down the lonesome
road, damp dollars stuck along the shoulder,

angel wings fresh-clipped. Most love's a code
to crack. Your lover's gone. And who comes back?

Lovely, Lonely

Her second beer's three-quarters gone. OK.
Not driving anywhere, just driving herself
crazy. Shostakovich on the playlist:
been her favorite lately, mournful with
some jokes thrown in. That amulet she bought
on Amazon's arrived: a Wiccan talisman
for poets, writers, actors. Can't hurt, right?
Looks lousy, rides too heavy on her neck.
Just like a spouse, like everything. "To be
like water, take the path of least resistance,
flow": a borrowed mantra that defaulted.
Broke, she'd like another loan: to purchase
"Death is just another door that opens." Calming
and sublime? The interest rate's too high.

Lullabies and Battle Cries

Small talk, the kind you say you hate, just think
of it as lullabies we sing to one
another, padding pain and easing us,
like Mother or a surrogate once did

or does, or otherwise we'd all be dead.
The skin along your cheek and neck and chest,
drum-taut for brush-like fingers, pulses from
within, a jazz band's riff, a battle cry

for tactics, acts, engagements, and improvisations
in love's name. Your liquid eyes burn dark
then light, fresh campsites on the night's hillside,
and circling round, the tribe, the fall and rise

of songs, the rhythm in the blood, the humming
rib bones of the whale that eats us all,
that feeds and cradles our next change, that spits
us out like seeds so bright the fires dim.

Luna

A beautiful cool night, clouds purple in
the silver moonlight, wind high in the gleaming
trees, she hears a shutter banging, rises,
wired, from bed.
                                    Her spouse asleep, the peaks
and valleys rising dull beneath the sheet,
but there's a mania—alive and feral—
in her mind.
                              She steps outside, back stoop
still warm from all-day summer sun, the scent
of side-yard flowers riding on the breeze.

And now a lovely form, a silver sliver
throbbing with her pulse, drifts ghostly over
all that backyard grass she mowed nine hours
ago.
      And suddenly, she feels her life,
its grind, the sprouting stump of it that's left.
She follows that strange silver glow straight through
the hedge's cleft. Yes, she'll return—but changed.

Midlife (II)

At last, as darkness falls,
you strip off all your clothes,
you walk in woods, the starlight
blue on skin, your breath
the only human sound,
and on and on, with snap
of twig and crackling leaves,
the moon once pulsing, now
a glow, a tablet melting
in a water glass,
your pain recedes, you feel
the waking beast inside,
heart wild with dream of claw
and fur and tooth, the scents
of musk and blood, not numbness
but raw howling all
along the aching instincts
you and night embrace.

Midlife (V)

Chorizo, couscous, thin-sliced gala apples
in a bowl: a bachelor's hash a husband
married many years can love, with spiky
jazz (that's Braxton morphing Monk), cold beer
in front of you. Your wife has turned in (headache),
so it's you and Trey, adopted greyhound
black as dreamless sleep. Linked memories,
your private myths—first Ali-Frazier fight
(on German radio), a gradeschool English
teacher and the story of his scar,
Andromeda's bare bottom in a painting
by Burne-Jones—rise glistening as boulders
in a river. Have you journeyed well
enough to know the boulders, be the river?

Nocturne (II)

You're in the kitchen, leaning on the counter,
beer in front of you, dog at your feet,
and trouble in your mind. Breasts pressed against
the sliding door, the darkness is a succubus,

inverted muse that has you disbelieving
that a deck is there, then shaggy spruces,
neighbor's house, the woods, the high school football
field, the university, downtown,

then M-14 and US-23,
the interstate, the road to anywhere,
perception's shadows decomposing so
damned fast you doubt the Earth, its curvature.

You listen to a record by an artist
that you love who's died, your heart a kite
in lightning that's been lurking in the wiry
wind. Your father gave you something in

a dream last night: you can't remember what.
No time for revelations now. Just ask
of what you've lost: Why did you leave? Where have
you gone? And are you ever coming back?

Sister

You're listening to Brahms and reading poems
on your phone, just hoping something warm
will light inside your head, because the weather
everywhere's too dark and cold. It's out
of season, out of joint, a tragedy,
if only life were more heroic. Wine
half gone, you've drawn a picture of a fox:
a journal sketch with ballpoint pen. A spirit
animal, your hippie friend would say.
On morning walks in nearby woods, you've seen
a fox. Last time, she caught your eye. You swear
she read the darkness in you, humped away
into the brush. So much like you: evasion
bears creation. Dare you call her sister?

Song of the Night

Light rain outside, and clouds within. Still groggy
from your reading: Homer's *Iliad*.
You asked for it. Your wife's on her computer,
dog is zonked. A load of laundry's going,
dishes in the sink. You've tried to be
a better husband, brother, lover, friend—
but what's that mean in middle age? And what's
been lost, reclaimed, or even gained? The payroll's
done, the penne's bubbling in the pot,
and Mahler's Seventh, Klemperer conducting,
soothes you through your earbuds. And? You wrote
a poem today. Materials and time:
still mastering the rudiments. What else?
You haven't died. The new roof will outlive you.

Staring at a Mirror's Back

You're using "you" in poems these days, the dreaded
second person. So, you've found no way
inside yourself—it's just like staring at
a mirror's back—and "you" might blast a path?
Each new day, you re-enact a dimly
lit creation myth. Ten thousand iterations
ought to do the trick: from chaos, to
an ever-morphing set of forms, to entropy.
The tragedies you love—*Macbeth* and *Lear*
and *Oedipus*—have given you a glimpse
of this, a life's small arc refined to art.
Last night, the burgers sizzling on the grill,
you sat cross-legged, oracular, and drank
a beer. The revelation: shadows, smoke.

Wolf Rune

The forest lands link earth with heaven,
spruce-tree tips like dendrites of elder earthen gods.

The long, dark, lonely winters swirl within
a song, the singer's storm-tossed mind at odds
with frozen lakes, the fir trees' needle-bed.

Moose-haunted evergreens stretch miles and miles,
and fallow fields will waken with the red
and purple flowers of the spring. The wiles

of ancient wolves weave through the singer's song,
the howls primeval, blood-bonds mingling, strong.

IV.

Anima

Almost eight billion living souls worldwide,
a Google search reveals. New trauma makes
her seek, then grim old schadenfreude shakes
her darker angel wide awake to guide
them to the black abyss's rim. "Jump in"
rides coldly on the wind. The frozen tears
she dreams grow wings like snow-spiked proteins, gears
the cosmic clock has shed to let time spin
like treadless tires on ice. "Death thins the herd,"
the flame-crowned demons murmur. Aching, pale,
she flies unaided in the haze. Lungs fail,
and eyes see darkly. Oh to speak one word.
She circles, soul crow-winged. Thoughts land to lope
and limp. And there—that feathered magic, Hope.

Devourers

Zen focus music oozing through the speakers.
You're all scattered: not just breaths, but thoughts
and feelings too. You're calling all those seekers:
poet, painter, dilettante that jots
and poses: gather energy, create.
The cosmos shimmers when they're active and
producing. Freed, you feed on them to sate
your need for deathlessness. No hourglass sand
will bury you, no unmarked grave will hold
you if you channel them to help you leave
a record: you, a maker, crazed and bold
enough to fashion artifacts that grieve
and laugh, that sing to their beholder, "I'm
alive," that stave off that devourer, Time.

The Green Flame

Enchanted eyes can see: the green flame burns
both day and night, glows inside, out. It keeps
the sky above, the sea behind, and turns
the woodland tides. It caws with ravens, sweeps
the dooryard, scares away the wolves and snakes,
and sings the dreaming children flowing songs
of evermore. It frames the mirrored lakes,
it bashes dawn's and sunset's brassy gongs,
and throbs eternal even under ghost-
blue palls of rainy days. It strokes the moon
to rosy glowing, sifts the clouds that coast
from roofs and parapets, and hides the rune
the proud and gauzy-headed fathers thought
they knew the secret name of, but do not.

Left to Darken

The tongueless temple bells swing silently
in cloisters of your mind. And you are blind,
the hero of a play that violently
emerged, full-formed, then flopped. No seer divined
apotheosis in a sequel. That's
fond hope. You can't have toiled so long to fade
to gray, then depthless black. But ladders, cats,
and other omens couldn't lie to staid
familiars you have courted, feared, fulfilled.
You sold the soiled soul you scraped from wheels
and treads of crumbling empires, those you've willed
to sons and daughters that your dark muse feels
were lucky to have not been born. No death
for them. But on your neck, you feel cold breath.

Migratory Goddesses

They've walked as half, down furrows in the south
of Iowa, up snowdrifts in the north,
Dakota, Massachusetts, Michigan,
at red tide in the Gulf, in Everglades,
through flood plains near the Rio Grande, the mouth
of the Missouri swelling, spewing forth
its silty kisses: Can they fish again?

And they have rolled their boulder, chained in Hades,
straight up and down a mountain, milk-filled breast
of the Eternal Feminine. They've dreamed
in fourteen pieces, cured in sand and sea,
crossed Styx to find themselves. They wander, dressed
in feathers, scales, or fur—their flesh star-seamed
where part of them's escaped, is dancing, free.

Persephone's First Spring

The hooves, claws, talons, boots have trampled all
your moon-chilled limbs, but you'll come back. And when
the pomegranate seeds explode, we'll call
the hibernating angels down. And then
we'll kiss, bite, lick the fruits, the grains, the flesh.
The dark pink buds, those jewels bedazzling crowns
of trees, will burst in silken petals, mesh
with spirits birthing moist new greens from browns.
Behind your ear, on down your neck, across
twin azimuths, your breasts, the bestial and
celestial intertwine. It's Hades' loss.
Earth's winds and rivers stroke the mud and sand
where you lie after nights you thought you'd die—
but now your stubbed wings sprout to let you fly.

Raquel, the Stars, the Moon

To fish for visions in the night, the sky
a pond that glitters overhead and all
around. To breathe this element, not die
or drown. To dive ascendingly, not fall.
Three wishes that entwine as one, she thinks,
the cooling night's dark velvet blue a balm
upon her flesh, a potion that she drinks
as old men drink *cervezas*, tanned and calm.
Her body beautified by work and sun,
her hands as strong as roots, as brown as bark,
yet gentle for her man and little one,
she's found this private moment in the dark,
a luscious chance to dream and hope, to love
and thank her god, a woman, there above.

Stay at Home

"I believe in you my soul," old Whitman
wrote. Your soul's been quarantined for decades,
flitting madly in the attic, drunk
on sump-pump swill. You wrote a poem Tuesday
with the simile "the soul expands
as if put on a ventilator." Sure.
Spring cleaning's what you need, but winter's caught
you napping: melting snow on tender tips
of spruces, bluejay squawking, feeder fallen
off the shepherd's crook. The coffee's gone,
too soon for beer or scotch. In bed, you read
a Polish poet whose name you can't pronounce.
Wife's made you fabric masks—one black, one blue—
to wear in public. "Bruised," she says. "So you."

April 2020

V.

Blue

Your mother's favorite color.
Joni's greatest record.
Sky
and sky
reflected in the water.
Unoxygenated blood.

A lonesomeness,
an inwardness,
a bruise,
sweet ache,
and easy riffing:

blue ribbon
blue pencil
blue collar
blue moon

the boys in blue
out of the blue
blue in the face
the wild blue yonder

true blue
blue blazes
Bluebeard
blue-haired lady

Kind of Blue
Midnight Blue
Blue Train
Two Steps from the Blues

blue note
blue spruce
blue movie
beaten black and blue

The skim-milk hue
of white folks' legs in summer.

"Too full o' th' milk
of human kindness."

Heaven.
And the stars that fleck
your one woke eye.

Dead Man's Quintet

i.

there's pasta water / boiling on the stove / "your poems are mush" / my darker angel murmurs / you'd think that wisdom / came with age / but I have only tropes / to slide around / dream lover's scalp / of hissing snakes / a pot of noodles / simmering

ii.

snow-salted branches like the gray in Dad's / hair while he lived this winter is a shaggy / spruce I'm shaggy too and we are sprucing / up the house by sorting winter clothes / and making piles of giveaways my wife's / got turtlenecks and sweaters stacked I offer / up four flowered shirts their brightness faded / styling out of date so much like me / a gauze-gray sky and every Friday black / my bedside-table catafalque of unread / books is gathering dust and casting shadow / listening to Brahms I miss Beethoven's edge / which makes me think I sharpen worn-down wisdom / wear the pearls or else they lose their luster

iii.

Trey trotting with me / now he squats two turds / lie steaming in the snow / a metaphor I fear exploring / I look up away instead / gray sky Midwestern winter / age has taught me / how to love each change / yes even my imagined final one / no hurry it will come / a string quartet is humming / through my headphones / the cello like a low-voiced / woman in my bed / I'm only here to dream iv.

sunshine and snowflakes come / and go awareness makes it so / and I am laboring / to make my strangled mind sky-sized / the book I'm reading now's / high modernism footnotes fragments / and allusions like a person / traumatized / reminds me of a horror / film I saw last May called *Men* / and this reminds me of / a supermarket shooting / of another at a church / and yes the cellist / in that playlist string quartet is sawing / pine-boards for my coffin

v.

she's cutting cookies trees and Santas / playlist rollicking snow blowing / like the ash of Armageddon / there's still a cup of coffee left / to bend my mind stop worrying / what day this is such drifting hard / to know how much has fallen sideways / flakes or floaters in my eyes / our thoughts aren't real remember this / mid-middle age its worry and / complacency complicity / in others' suffering as well / I'm hardly tragic actually / already dead I wonder just / how long it's been right all my life

First Time You Meet Her Parents

grass stains on your jeans, / hung over, glasses missing, / queasy over diner pancakes, butter, maple / syrup, carried home / like Dionysus (student / in you writes) the night / before, a woman on / each side, you nursing new / and old imagined wounds, / your hand atremble on / the coffee cup, you want / to kiss her, meds not kicking / in, self-consciousness / impossible to shake, / a tick dug in between / your shoulder blades, inherent / in the metaphor / is blood, wide river you / will travel on with her / for days then months then years, / but first the grayheads: Hi.

Folly

i.

I lived in Iowa / when dad was / in Vietnam. / I asked him later / if he killed anyone. / He told me you could never tell: / such smoke and chaos. / Lack of vision. / I don't think he used these words. / It's just my memory / that decorates, useless / as the Purple Heart / he was awarded but / never got— / the ocular proof, / as that good soldier, / Othello, says.

ii.

I was a whale / in the ocean / of my mother. / Leviathan, I / swallowed all. / Breached, breathing, / naming, aging / since. / These are only markers, / harpoons / in the flesh / of sentience.

iii.

I've been re-reminded lately / that my thoughts / aren't real. / They're clouds / or falling leaves. / Angels. / Demons. / I see them. / I can grab them. / I can encompass them. / They are not me / but / products I create. / They could be art. They could be / commerce. They could be / trash. They are / compostable, I think.

Gold

Metallic yellow
Ripened grain
The setting and the rising sun
Teeth-fillings of the elders
Ingots in Fort Knox
The dust and nuggets panned from mountain streams
Dad's jaundiced eyes in 1967 Vietnam
My hair when I was young
My mother's, sisters', wife's worn wedding rings
The lesson of King Midas

It's drifting in some rare champagnes
And fancy restaurants will dust their hamburgers with it

I spent my youth near cornfields
Spent my youth near people's yellow teeth
And what that's done
Both for and to me

Good as gold
Belief in linking wealth with worth
A country song goes, "You're as good as gold/And I'm as good as gone"
Some toxic positivity at play
I'll ask my younger, hipper, blonder poet friend, KD

The sun is like a yolk
A yolk is just an embryo
An embryo I've been
My momma's golden boy
Her one and lonely son

White Spaces

i.

you try so hard to make the ideal real
but really you're just tracing   tracks on snowy
sidewalks   drips in dim mind-alleys of
the betters that you trust   such trysts   now music
cool and minimal pours vodka-clear
from wireless speakers   wife is gone   a ball
game's on TV   you're drinking beer   relax
six decades of your life are in the can
and night has cast its spell   the windows echo
mirrors of all vanity   oh well
the love you make   the love you take   the Beatles
why are they your favorite   it's mouthfeel
maybe   but with Dylan   they made art
of pop   you've only planted seeds in snow

ii.

you think you'll make another one   or love
another one   or live another one
clichés and pop Romanticism   read
or meditate   or try this metaphor
go shoot your ego in the head   and finish
that damn beer and cook some food   two ears
and one fat mouth   so listen   weigh your options
weight your big head down   and wait before

you speak or make   now Arvo Pärt is on
the playlist   crystalline white space   such whiteness
haunts so many   words of Blake and Melville
clear your mind's debris   tabula rasa
belly of your spouse   blank page or screen
an open field   a veined hand on the plow

Widening Stage

i.

This love's a widening stage, with acts and scenes, / and we've been moving props for many years: / the Army blanket, shroud of Vietnam, / that we made love on, summer nights outdoors; / my parents' bed, a hand-me-down, so creepy, / cost-effective; fold-out sofa too.

ii.

These words? The Chorus merely, footnote to / a memoir we will never write. The audience / must use its own imagination. "Comedy / embraces tragedy": we'll go with that. / "The grave's a fine and private place, but none, / I think, do there embrace": yes, fair enough.

iii.

But nothing physical is ever really / lost. It's scattered, recombined: the scent / of vodka, blood, deodorant. There's usually / an epilogue, but science tells us now / the scenes lay out like tarot cards: a widening / reality, the one we sometimes feel / but often fail to see. —Kiss me, at least.

www.ingramcontent.com/pod-product-compliance
Lightning Source LLC
Chambersburg PA
CBHW022201160726
48282CB00024B/271
* 9 7 8 8 1 1 9 2 2 8 8 9 8 *